Trams & Recollections
Sunderland Trams in the

David Clarke

First published in 2017

British Library Cataloguing in Publication Data

A catalogue record for this book is available from the British Library.

ISBN 978 1 85794 513 3

Silver Link Publishing Ltd
The Trundle
Ringstead Road
Great Addington
Kettering
Northants NN14 4BW

Tel/Fax: 01536 330588
email: sales@nostalgiacollection.com
Website: www.nostalgiacollection.com

Printed and bound in the Czech Republic

The following books have been of help in compiling the captions for this photographic collection, and are recommended to anyone wishing to gain further information on Sunderland's tram system:

Staddon, S. A. *The Tramways of Sunderland* (The Sunderland Echo)
Irwin, Christopher R. *A Nostalgic Look at North East Trams Since the 1940s* (Silver Link Publishing, ISBN 978-0-947971-45-9)
Lockwood, Stephen *Trams Across the Wear* (Adam Gordon, ISBN 978-1-874422-76-1)

Title page: On a dull day in November 1952 a former Manchester 'Pilcher' car in Ryhope Road approaches the junction with Villette Road on the right. The trams on Villette Road had been withdrawn two years before, and this is the last day for the Grangetown route. *R.J.S. Wiseman.*

Front cover: No 93 crosses the Monkwearmouth Bridge on 15 June 1954. This tram was one of a batch of nine cars built by EEC in 1934, known as 'Wearsiders'. The bridge was opened on 31 October 1929 by the Duke of York (later King George VI) at a cost of more than £230,000. It was fabricated by the firm of Sir William Arrol & Co at its Dalmarnock ironworks in Glasgow – the company also built the Forth Road Bridge and the steel structure of Tower Bridge in London. The van behind the tram belongs to the Central Laundry in Sunderland, which has a long history, being first established in 1887. *Peter Mitchell*

David Clarke was born in London in August 1936, living there and travelling to school on trams and trolleybuses until 1952. Four years as an engineering trainee with the Westinghouse Brake & Signal Company was followed by becoming an engineering undergraduate at the University of Leeds. Switching from engineering to teaching Physics and Mathematics, David ultimately was the Head of Science for 17 years at a Leeds comprehensive school. In 1983 he obtained an MSc in Physics Education at the University of York. A lifelong interest in transport in general, and trams in particular, has enabled him to present this brief but hopefully interesting work on the trams of Sutherland.

Introduction

Sunderland's trams had an appeal to tram enthusiasts that was as great as any other British system. Possibly it was the fact that many were second-hand from other systems, or was it their (almost unique) pantographs in their later years?

Like many others, I was fascinated by trams from an early age. I can remember looking out of the first-floor front window of our house (we lived above a shop where my father was manager) and noticing not the few motor cars, which were all black, or the trade vans, or even the fairly ordinary shops and houses, but the brightly coloured red and cream trams that seemed to pass by every few minutes. This was North London, not Sunderland, but the effect would have been the same anywhere. Trams were the conspicuous things, and they were beautiful to behold. When I was just short of two years old they were taken away and trolleybuses substituted, and I can remember asking my mother what had happened to them. The trolleys somehow did not command the presence that the trams had held.

My first visit to Sunderland was in February 1953. I spent the day riding the trams and securing a few photographs of them. The memory of that first ride to Seaburn (Sealane) in the glorious midday sunshine will stick forever. And those elegant centre-entrance cars! I later discovered similar trams in Blackpool and Aberdeen, but these were my first experience of something quite modern.

The reason (or excuse) for producing yet another book of Sunderland tram photographs is the recent discovery of the excellent collection of the late Peter Mitchell. Peter was a friend of mine who lived close by in North London and we occasionally met up at my home or went on public transport visits together. Peter was working and could afford a good camera; I was on pocket money and had a cheap box camera. So it is Peter's superb pictures, and some views by Clarence Carter, that are presented here, together with 11 of Richard Wiseman's excellent photographs, which he has kindly allowed me to use. I am so grateful to Hugh Taylor for his painstaking work in sorting Peter's photographs and details of his notes, and to Henry Conn for his generous willingness to scan the negatives, because without their efforts this selection would not be possible. Henry also provided much detail for the captions from his own research. Thanks also to Roger Smith for producing a most excellent map of the system showing the locations of the photographs.

And just a word about the full-page pictures – when viewing a scene naturally one is conscious of about a 50° angle of vision (although only a small fraction of this is sharp). To look at a small picture on a page is like standing back from a window through which one is looking, your angle of view is reduced and you don't feel in the scene. Holding a full-page picture at 40cm or so from your eye (normal reading distance) gives you something approaching the natural 50° viewing angle – you feel more as though you are there.

The time will come when all of us who remember the first-generation British tramscape will have departed. So we want to share with others our treasured memories of an age when life was less dominated by the motor car. Yes, we did not have the convenience of modern digital technology and many other comforts of modern living, but we had the trams, and we loved them, and they were a fixture in the streets that seemed so permanent. Sadly they were not so permanent due to the attitude of transport authorities, which put short-term financial benefits above long-term quality investments. Thankfully the tram, with its excellent qualities of quick loading and high capacity, delivering us to the streets where we want to be, is making a return to British towns and cities, and may one day reach Sunderland.

This book is not a definitive history of the trams or the system – for those works see the excellent publications of S. A. Staddon and Stephen Lockwood, details of which are in the Bibliography. This book is just sheer nostalgia. It is hoped that it will have appeal not only to tram enthusiasts but also to locals (and ex-locals) of Sunderland who remember the trams, and the streets they ran in, before the great Motor Car Age arrived.

Sunderland's tram system never grew to fill the city. Had it been extended from Southwick to the estates on the Washington Road, and up the Chester Road to Pennywell and Grindon, up the Hylton Road to South Hylton, from Kayll Road to Pallion and from Grangetown to Ryhope (where the former Sunderland District trams went), there might have been a much stronger case for retention. As it was, all these areas were served by buses. The last tramway extension was from Humbledon to Thorney Close on an excellent central reservation. It could have gone another mile to reach Middle and East Herrington, although street running would have been necessary for the final stretch. The recent reintroduction of trams to places like Nottingham and Manchester shows what a difference to the ambience of a town or city a clean and accessible tram system can be. Sunderland has the Metro, but we need something between that and the very useful bus. Perhaps before long spending on transport improvements will be recognised as a valuable investment in our health and environment.

David Clarke
Hamsterley
County Durham

System map

The numbers accompanying each caption refer to the locations marked on the map of the system

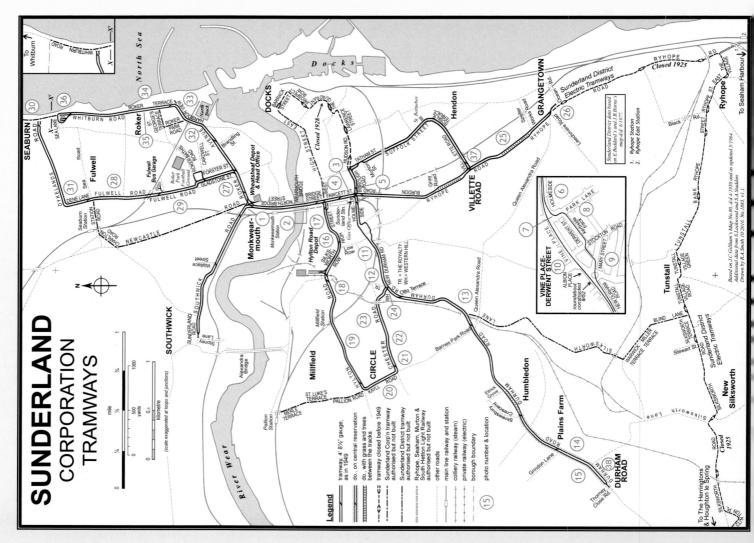

SUNDERLAND CORPORATION TRAMWAYS

Legend

	tramway 4' 8½" gauge, as in 1949
	do., on central reservation
	do., with grass and trees between the tracks
	tramway closed before 1949
	Sunderland Corp'n tramway authorised but not built
	Sunderland District tramway authorised but not built
	Ryhope, Seaham, Murton & South Hetton Light Railway authorised but not built
	other roads
	main line railway and station
	colliery railway (steam)
	private railway (electric)
	borough boundary
(15)	photo number & location

(scale exaggerated at loops and junctions)

Based on J.C.Gillham's Map No.80, d/d 4/1950 and as updated 5/1964. Additional data from S.J.Lockwood and S.A.Staddon. Drawn by R.A.Smith 10/2016. No.1883, v1.1

Sunderland District data based on E.Beddard's and J.B.Horne's map d/d 6/1977.

1. Ryhope Station
2. Ryhope East Station

① On 10 September 1952, sitting at The Wheatsheaf on the truncated track that formerly led to Southwick, is ex-Huddersfield No 32, about to do a shortworking on the Durham Road route. The private car is of similar age to the tram and also comes from Yorkshire. *R. J. S. Wiseman*

2 No 15 is here approaching the Monkwearmouth Bridge. This tram was originally an open-top bogie car built in 1900, but was rebuilt to the four-wheel enclosed style seen here in 1920 and 1934. Today the overhead wires have disappeared from the right-hand bridge and appeared on the left-hand one, which carries the Metro. *Clarence Carter*

3 Binns department store in Fawcett Street was advertised on the ends of every tram and bus in the Corporation Transport fleet (how much did that cost the firm?). Here No 87 passes the store on the rather wet afternoon of 14 June 1954. The shoppers are still about despite the weather. *Peter Mitchell*

Heading for

③ Grangetown in Fawcett Street, the city's main shopping street, is No 53, from 1936, the first with the ends in the Blackpool style, similar to No 99. *Clarence Carter*

4 A busy scene in Fawcett Street on 10 September 1952. No 32 is an ex-Huddersfield tram and is followed by an ex-Manchester car. The Huddersfields were robust and outlasted the Manchesters. *R. J. S. Wiseman*

⑤   No 99 was a superb tram with a high capacity, built by EEC in 1935. There is a good load downstairs here in Borough Road, and it is travelling to the Hendon district where it will terminate at Villette Road. Unfortunately No 99 and its sister bogie car No 100, an ex-London 'Feltham', were found to be expensive to run and in later years saw only occasional use at busy times. *Clarence Carter*

⑥   No 94 loads in Holmside for Humbledon. This was the original terminus for the Durham Road trams before the final extension to Thorney Close Road and was frequently used for short workings. This batch of cars was built by English Electric in 1933 and, although the design was a little dated, they became the mainstay of this route. *Clarence Carter*

⑥ A good number of intending passengers are about to board No 5 (ex-Ilford) at the same location on its way to Durham Road. *Clarence Carter*

⑦ No 52 was the newest car built for Sunderland in 1940 with Blackpool-type ends. On 5 September 1953 it is seen rounding the curve from Holmside into Park Lane. A Morris Minor sits outside the 'Beehive' pub. As can be seen in the 'present-day' view, by 2016 the lovely 'Beehive' and Tates have gone. *R. J. S. Wiseman/author*

⑧ *Right:* With Park Lane in the background, ex-Huddersfield car No 35 enters Derwent Street, part of the outward single-track section, on 17 June 1953. The Huddersfield cars never had the lower front dash painted with the curve-sided cream 'triangle' that adorned the rest of the fleet. *Peter Mitchell*

(9) The outbound one-way tram track is seen again in the narrow Derwent Street at its junction with Mary Street on 5 September 1953. Tram 83 was built by EEC in 1921-22 for Sunderland.

The back end of Chaplins pub has not changed today, but the garage has given way to a Wetherspoons establishment. Note the extended pavement, ornamental lamp and litter bin. *R. J. S. Wiseman/author*

10 Car 8 was an ex-Ilford car bought by Sunderland in 1937, and is seen here on 17 June 1953 on the inbound single-track section passing the ornate facade of the Technical College building in Vine Place. This section was the counterpart to Derwent Street used by outbound cars, seen in the previous pictures. The tram is being followed by a 'Northern' SE4 bus with an English Electric body, built around 1939. *Peter Mitchell*

(11) Not much other than the right hand bridge parapet remains today in this view at the railway bridge in New Durham Road, having all been swept away to provide roads for the all-conquering motor vehicle. In more peaceful days No 42 (ex-Manchester) is on the Circle route on 5 September 1953. *R. J .S. Wiseman*

12 Car 8 is in the older part of Durham Road at Fox Street on 17 June 1953. The window-cleaner at work is unaware that he is being recorded for posterity!
The adverts on the terrace end may bring back memories for some. *Peter Mitchell*

(13)   On the same day a rather daring bus driver is caught overtaking on the offside of No 24 in the Durham Road at Barnes Park, probably due to there being
no other traffic about. No 24 was rebuilt by Sunderland from a Mansfield District tram in 1934. The bus is a Roe-bodied AEC Regent built in 1950 for
Sunderland & District. *Peter Mitchell*

(14) No 87 was one of the mainstay batch of trams built by the English Electric company in 1933, and worked the Durham Road route until the end of that line. It is seen here, also on 17 June 1953, at Grindon Lane. The central reservation enabled good timekeeping to be maintained. *Peter Mitchell*

15 No 8 is one of the ex-London (Ilford) trams, seen on that same June day on the Durham Road reserved track at North Moor, just short of the line's terminus.

The housing has now been developed much nearer the road, and the reservation lies unused while the buses of today occupy road space – which seems to be a planning mistake.
Peter Mitchell

(15)   This beautiful tram –
No 52 – was built in
Sunderland in 1940 and was
the final product of the Hylton
Road works. It is seen here
outside the Londonderry Hotel
on 14 June 1953 at about 4
o'clock in the afternoon. In
2016 the road outside the
Londonderry is pedestrianised
– and deserted! *Peter Mitchell/
author*

(17) Car No 41 was one of six bought from Manchester in 1947, having been built in 1930 and known as 'Pilchers' after the manager who commissioned them. Here it is seen in High Street West on 10 September 1952. A funeral procession is held up while the tram loads passengers. *R. J. S. Wiseman*

18   An almost deserted Hylton Road at Deptford Road is where No 22 is seen on 14 June 1953, heading into town where it will terminate. The Circle route was not quite a complete circle, more like a question-mark shape. Many roads were paved with stone setts, which sometimes left gaps near the rails when in poor condition. *Peter Mitchell*

(19) No 22 is at the Willow Pump in Hylton Road on 14 June 1953 – note the Coronation bunting. This tram started life as a single-decker in 1901, being rebuilt as a double-decker in 1925. It is heading away from town, going the long way round back to town via Kayll Road, then out to Roker. The bus behind is No 126, a Roe-bodied Daimler CVG6 built in 1951.
Peter Mitchell

(20)   On the same day tram No 13 is at the west end of Kayll Road, with Chester
        Road at right angles at the traffic signals ahead. No 13 started life in 1900 but
was thoroughly rebuilt throughout its life, one result being the mismatch between
the upper and lower deck windows. Kayll Road is now part of the busy ring road,
but the shelter on the left survives! *Peter Mitchell/author*

(21) Outside the hospital in Chester Road, No 49, the first of the third type of modern car (built in 1938), is the only vehicle around on that same June day. 'Powleys Sparkling Drinks' was a common advert on the sides of the centre-entrance cars, being a local Sunderland company founded in the late 19th century. The tram has just gone past a section breaker, a feed point for the supply to the overhead wires. *Peter Mitchell*

22 No 51 is in Chester Road at Eldon Street on 10 September 1952, on its way to Roker via the town centre, forming the return route of the 'Circle' trams. These splendid vehicles brightened up drab streets when, as in this case, they were freshly cleaned. *R. J. S. Wiseman*

(24) *Right:* On 17 June 1953 a lightly loaded No 87 is heading for town from the Durham Road and has arrived at the junction with Western Hill (on the left) at The Royalty (behind the tram). The Circle route goes off to the left.

Looking in a slightly different direction (into Western Hill) in 2016 we can see that the corner shop and first house on the right have gone, and those on the left cut back. *Peter Mitchell/ author*

(23) No 36 is an ex-Huddersfield tram and is seen here in Chester Road at Hylton Street on 14 June 1953. It is going towards town and will then go out to Roker and Seaburn (Sealane). The shops are still there today but have changed hands and been considerably modernised. *Peter Mitchell*

(25)   With a mad scramble to
        board, and a lady running to
catch it, No 23, on its way inwards
from Grangetown, stops at Weldon
Avenue, Ryhope Road, on 10
September 1952. Ahead of the tram
the road becomes dual carriageway
with the tracks laid on either side of
the centre tree-lined strip.
    Not much has changed here
in the intervening years – just the
tracks, poles and wires have gone. *R. J.
S. Wiseman/author*

26 The array of nine advertisements on the wall of the house is a study in itself – one wonders if anyone would stand still long enough to read them all! But the tram is also interesting – No 38 is an ex-Manchester 'Pilcher', bought by Sunderland in 1947; it has just left the Grangetown terminus on 30 November 1952 and is heading for The Wheatsheaf at the far end of the town. *R. J. S. Wiseman*

27 *Left:* No 80, built in 1921-22 by English Electric and retrucked in 1929 by the Corporation, is seen in the narrow Gladstone Street on 17 June 1953. Before the days of town-centre and out-of-town supermarkets, the corner shop was an absolute essential to the life of the community. Note the advert for Ben Ewe whisky, a local brew. *Peter Mitchell*

28 *Right:* No 27 was one of three splendid cars built by the Corporation in 1935, the first modern vehicles with glass roof panels. On 10 September 1952 it has stopped ahead of some track repair works at Millview Avenue, Fulwell Road, on its way to Seaburn. *R. J. S. Wiseman*

(29)   *Above:* No 8, an ex-London (Ilford) car, is in Fulwell Road at Osbourne Street on 17 June 1953, on its way to Durham Road via the town centre. These cars were some of the mainstays of this route. Built by the Brush company in 1932, they were rather dated in appearance but must have been well made as they lasted to the end of the system. *Peter Mitchell*

(30) At the Dykelands Road, Seaburn, terminus, also on 17 June 1953, No 96, a Sunderland Corporation-built tram of 1934, stands awaiting a return to Durham Road via the town. Although only a few hundred yards from the Whitburn Road terminus, the two sets of tracks were never connected. *Peter Mitchell*

(31) One of the ex-London (Ilford) cars, No 9, is seen on the same day in Dykelands Road at Dacre Road, with typical suburban semis. Plenty of ventilation is provided for the lower saloon by the scoops above the main windows, and there were no platform doors! *Peter Mitchell*

(32) No 85 is in Harbour View, Roker, on that same June day. This tram was bought from Bury Corporation in 1948 and was an extensive rebuild of a 1905 vehicle. Just why the Corporation chose this single vehicle is unknown – there were probably better bargains on the market. *Peter Mitchell*

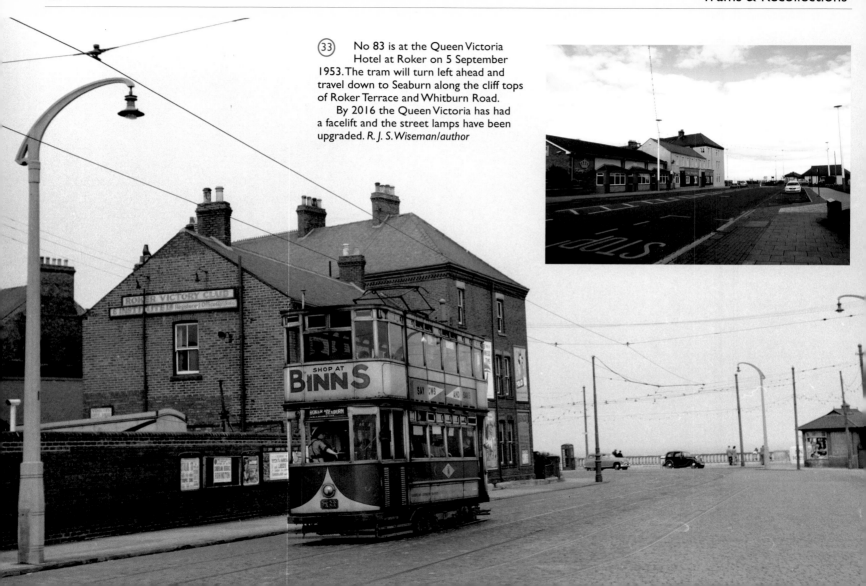

(33) No 83 is at the Queen Victoria Hotel at Roker on 5 September 1953. The tram will turn left ahead and travel down to Seaburn along the cliff tops of Roker Terrace and Whitburn Road.

By 2016 the Queen Victoria has had a facelift and the street lamps have been upgraded. *R. J. S. Wiseman/author*

(34) No 77 is an English Electric car of 1921-22 and is seen here discharging passengers at Roker Terrace. It still has a good load on board, probably going to the terminus at Sealane just a few stops further on. The scene is much the same today but without the tram, poles, wires and tracks. *Clarence Carter*

35 On a slightly sea-misty 17 June 1953, No 55 comes up Roker Terrace from the Seaburn (Sealane) terminus, heading for town and the Chester Road 'Circle' route. Built by the Brush company in 1935-36, this was one of a pair of attractive modern cars that followed the Nos 26-28 batch. *Peter Mitchell*

(36) No photographic survey of Sunderland's tramways could possibly omit a view of the Seaburn (Sealane) terminus. Sometimes on hot sunny days in the summer several trams at a time could be seen here. No 63 was one of the oldest in the fleet in the 1950s, having been rebuilt in 1933 from a 1902 open-topper. It is seen here on a dull 17 June 1953, when the crowds were absent. *Peter Mitchell*

SHOP AT BINNS

CIRCLE

85

SHOP AT BINNS
90

(36) This is No 85, one of the front-exit trams rebuilt in 1930 and seen here at Sealane terminus about to negotiate the turning loop before unloading. The bus behind is well loaded and going further.

Today the well-loved terminus at Sealane is just a through bus stop, but the substantial shelter remains.
Clarence Carter/author

(38) This is the terminus of the Durham Road reserved track extension completed in 1949, the last line to be built. Car 98, one of the mainstays of this route and the highest numbered, waits to return to Seaburn on 17 June 1953. *Peter Mitchell*

(37)   Ex-Manchester car 42 is seen at the Villette Road
       terminus; the date and photographer are
unknown, but if anyone can supply any details please
contact the author via the publisher. Photographs on this
and the Southwick route are rather more difficult to find
as the trams were removed from them in 1950 and 1951
respectively. An even earlier closure, in 1928, was the
short route to the docks.

Epilogue

Memories are precious things and
photographs are a wonderful help to
refreshing them. We like to remember
the good things – the quieter streets,
slower pace of life, perhaps more
intimate family gatherings and so on,
while overlooking the memories of
cold bedrooms in winter (and unheated
trams and buses), less appetising food,
widespread body odour and the sheer
hard graft of housework and poor
workplace conditions. It is not sensible
to pretend that the old days were better,
and we cannot hold onto those things
that are inevitably unable to remain part
of living in the present age, however much we
miss them.

       The trams of Sunderland (and any town or
city) were essentially part of the place, much
more so than buses, simply because the tracks
and wires remained when the tram had left.
The tram had a long life, especially if constantly
upgraded, but this was often the cause of
its demise – there was too much left of the
original, so it appeared dated. In the 1950s
Sunderland had a mixture of quite antiquated

and smart modern vehicles. But it was also the
track layout that often offended the motorist,
who was then encouraged to think that his
conveyance was the most important – if the
tram got in his way, then the tram had to go.

       Thankfully public transport has risen in the
estimation of many town and city dwellers, and
in an increasing number of places good-quality
public transport is becoming an essential
investment. The motorist is now feeling the
restrictions – there is simply not enough space
for us all to drive through the city streets.

The tram is making a return, its large carrying
capacity, rapid loading and unloading through
multiple doors at street level and ultra-smooth
ride making it very attractive. In addition, it
keeps pollution off the streets. So we may yet
see a reincarnation of the tram in Sunderland,
although it will look very different from those
pictured in this book.

       Finally, if you recognise yourself or your
relatives or friends in any of these pictures, just
jump for joy – and if you can let the author
know, he will be as pleased as you!